# YOUR MIND IS CHANGED:

**A practical guide to mind mastery, overcoming negativity and finding happiness.**

**MICHEAL MURRAY**

# Table of Contents

# Chapter 1

**Why We Think**

The brain is a survival mechanism. One of the key reasons humans have survived for so long is because we are masters of adaptability.

The ideas in our minds are typically thought of as part of ourselves. They are, in a way. There are two sorts of thinking. We have conscious thinking (thoughts that you control) and unconscious thoughts (thoughts that you do not control) (thoughts that you do not control). If you can conceive of it as your lungs, it's quite comparable. You may deliberately breathe, but while you're doing other things, you're unintentionally breathing.

The rationale for these unconscious thoughts is to evaluate risk. You see, the brain has a very great thing it does. You have blind patches in your field of vision. Your brain takes the information surrounding the location and physically fills it in with information so that there are no gaps in your view.

So, what this indicates is that your mind is relatively independent.

When you encounter a stranger, your brain will instantly develop a tale for that person based on what it sees, and what has occurred to you in the past, particularly if it was something horrific. This is your brain's survival mechanism. So, all these ideas that spring up are your brain "guessing" what is occurring.

This may throw some individuals into problems since it just so happens that some people accept these notions as real. This is called judging and presuming.

The prefrontal cortex, which is the newest development in evolution, is how you consciously govern things. In reality, the prefrontal cortex truly is still in development until the mid to late 20s. This is what experts think drives teens to behave more impulsively and recklessly. Now, we don't know precisely where in the prefrontal cortex the awareness is situated, but we know that this area of the brain can regulate things consciously.

So, the reason we think as we do is that the brain wants to live, but also that people are unique enough to form ideas and place their own opinions on what those thoughts are. It's really extremely great.

Cognitive psychologists have made tremendous progress in describing how humans think. However, very little time and attention have been devoted to studying why we think—the elements that make us start or stop thinking, pick and alter tactics and solutions. Such issues are connected to motivation and discriminative and reinforcing stimuli. The premise is that examining thinking as a sort of action tightly tied to antecedent stimuli and outcomes leads to potentially significant topics that are not now being explored in the area of cognitive psychology. This is not an argument for returning to behaviorism—rather, the claim is made that incorporating a behavioral viewpoint on thinking will improve cognitive psychology.

Most of us have had someone remark, "Think positive!" or "Look on the bright side," when things didn't go quite right. As tough as it may be to hear, there is some truth behind it. Positive thinking may lower your stress level, make you feel better about yourself (and the circumstances), and enhance your general well-being and attitude.

The only difficulty is that it's not always simple to remain optimistic, and certain conditions make it more of a struggle than others. The good news: With a little practice in turning around your negative thinking, you can become an optimist.

The Attitudes of Optimists and Pessimists

Research demonstrates the advantages of optimism and a happy attitude of mind are substantial. Optimists have better health, healthier relationships, are more productive, and suffer less stress, among other things.

This is because optimists prefer to take greater chances. They also blame external conditions if they fail, retaining a "try again" mentality.

Because of their resilience, optimists are more likely to succeed in the future and less disturbed by failure in general.

Pessimists, on the other hand, tend to blame themselves when things go wrong and grow more hesitant to try again with each unpleasant event in life. They begin to look at happy occurrences in their lives as "flukes" that have little to do with them and anticipate the worse.

In this sense, optimists and pessimists alike construct self-fulfilling promises.

Your Perception of Negative Events When you understand how both outlooks interpret situations, it becomes evident how optimism and positive self-talk may affect your stress levels, as can pessimism and negative self-talk.

Negative situations are less distressing when you regard them as "not your fault" and less likely to repeat. Similarly, happy experiences are especially sweeter when you regard them as proof of more to come and consider yourself the ruler of your destiny. Because of the difference in behavior, people who routinely practice positive thinking tend to enjoy greater success, which may add up to a less stressful existence.

How to Learn to Be Optimistic
How can you utilize this knowledge to lessen your stress level? Fortunately, optimism can be learned. With practice, you can modify your self-talk (your inner dialogue, what you say to yourself about what you're feeling) and your explanatory style (the unique ways

that optimists and pessimists absorb their experiences) (the specific ways that optimists and pessimists process their experiences). Here's how:

Take the Optimism Self Test.
Learn if you're an optimist or a pessimist and to what degree. The reason why this is significant is that many pessimists believe they're optimists; nonetheless, optimism is characterized by particular criteria. If you know where you stand on the optimism-pessimism continuum, you'll have a better notion of what may require change.

Try to be positive.
Once you understand your current way of seeing things, you may make a deliberate effort to look at things differently when you're confronted with scenarios. Now is the ideal moment to practice various sorts of positive self-talk and learn how to become an optimist.

Use Positive Affirmations.
You may reprogram yourself and your way of thinking by employing positive affirmations daily. This will assist optimistic thinking to become more automatic. Over time, you will have to intentionally think less about it when each new circumstance comes along.

What Is Positive Thinking?
What precisely is positive thinking? You could be tempted to conclude that it entails viewing the world through rose-colored spectacles by disregarding or glossing over the bad parts of life. However, positive thinking essentially implies tackling life's obstacles with a positive viewpoint.
Positive thinking does not necessarily imply avoiding or dismissing the terrible things of life. Instead, it entails making the most of potentially terrible circumstances, striving to see the best in other people, and seeing yourself and your talents from a positive perspective.

Optimistic explaining style: People with an optimistic explanatory style prefer to give themselves credit when positive things happen and often blame outside sources for unfavorable results. They also tend to regard unfavorable occurrences as fleeting and uncommon.

Pessimistic explanation style: On the other hand, people with a pessimistic explanatory style generally blame themselves when terrible things happen, but fail to give themselves due credit for beneficial results. They also have a propensity to regard unpleasant experiences as anticipated and persistent. As you can guess, blaming yourself for occurrences beyond your control or considering these terrible events as a continuous part of your life may have a severe influence on your state of mind.

Positive thinkers are more prone to utilize an optimistic explication style, but the method in which individuals attribute events might also differ depending upon the precise scenario. For example, a person who is normally an optimistic thinker could employ a more pessimistic explanation style in exceptionally trying conditions, such as at work or school.

While numerous elements affect whether a person has a happy view, how they explain the events of their life, known as their explanatory style, plays an essential effect.

Positive Psychology vs. Positive Thinking
While the phrases "positive thinking" and "positive psychology" are frequently used interchangeably, it is vital to clarify that they are not the same thing. Positive thinking is about looking at things from a positive point of view. It is a kind of thinking that focuses on keeping a happy, optimistic mindset. Positive psychology is a discipline of psychology that explores the consequences of optimism, what produces it, and when it is best exploited.

Positive Thinking Has Health Benefits

In recent years, the so-called "power of positive thinking" has acquired a significant amount of attention owing to self-help publications such as "The Secret." While these pop-psychology publications frequently pitch positive thinking as a type of psychological cure, empirical research has demonstrated that there are many very genuine health advantages associated with positive thinking and optimistic attitudes.

Positive thinking is connected to a broad variety of health benefits, including:

- Better stress management and coping skills
- Enhanced psychological wellbeing
- Greater resistance to the common cold
- Increased physical well-being
- A longer life span
- Lower rates of depression
- Reduced risk of cardiovascular disease-related death

One study of 1,558 older people indicated that positive thinking might potentially improve frailty throughout old age.

A 2018 study published in the Journal of Aging Research indicated that having a good mental attitude was connected to lower mortality across 35 years. People who had a more optimistic view were also more likely to obtain regular physical activity, avoid smoking, eat a better diet, and receive higher quality sleep.

There are numerous advantages to positive thinking, but why precisely does positive thinking have such a profound influence on physical and mental health?

One argument is that those who think positively tend to be less influenced by stress. Research reveals that having more positive automatic thoughts helps individuals become more robust in the face of life's harsh situations. People who had high levels of positive thinking were more likely to come away from stressful life situations with a better sense of the meaningfulness of life.

Another possibility is that people who think positively tend to live healthier lives in general; they may exercise more, follow a more nutritious diet, and avoid unhealthy behaviors.

How to Practice Positive Thinking
While you may be more prone to negative thinking, there are tactics that you can apply to become a more optimistic thinker. Practicing these tactics frequently might help you get into the habit of keeping a more optimistic view of life.

Notice your thoughts: Start paying attention to the sort of ideas you experience each day. If you realize that many of them are negative, make a deliberate effort to reframe how you are thinking more positively.

Write in a thankfulness journal: Practicing gratitude may have a variety of good advantages, and it can help you learn to have a better attitude. Experiencing thankful feelings enables individuals to feel more positive.

Use positive self-talk: How you talk to yourself can play an important role in shaping your outlook. Studies have shown that shifting to more positive self-talk can have a positive impact on your emotions and how you respond to stress. The Small Changes to Changing Your Habits and Lifestyle Without Suffering for Bigger Results = (Quick Strength Training Workouts + Weekly Diet Challenges and Healthy Weight Loss)

# Chapter 2

**Focussing on what you can control**

The tension we all deal with on a day-to-day basis is much to bear. For better or worse, many things in our lives are beyond our control. However, if you spend all of your energy on the things you can't control instead of placing the focus on what you can manage, you'll probably feel even more stressed out - like you have no control over your own life. However, this is not the case. Believe it or not, there are a handful of extremely essential things you can control in life. If you concentrate on what you can manage, you may alter your perspective for the better, resulting in a more optimistic view of life and a can-do attitude.

Here are four methods to concentrate on what you can control.

1. Focus on What You Can Control by Making a List

The first step to concentrating on what you can control is to develop a list of "things I can control." When you take a step back and compile this list, you'll likely find that you have a lot more power than you anticipated.

Here are some suggestions to add to your "Things I Can Control" list.

Your attitude: While we can't control what occurs to us, we can manage our attitude towards these situations. For example, let's imagine you're delayed in traffic and late for work. When these external elements are in control of your circumstances, one of the few things you can influence is your attitude. Are you going to lose your cool and have zero tolerance, for cursing the drivers around you? Or, are you going to say, "it is what it is" and simply enjoy the music or podcast you're listening to?

Your effort: Whether it's at business or in your personal life, you control the effort you put in. Focus on what you can manage by having a can-do attitude and putting your maximum effort into all you do. You can't control the outcomes of circumstances, but when you manage what you can control - your effort – you can raise the odds of having a great result.

Your breath: While we breathe 24/7 without even thinking about it, we do have the potential to zero in on our breath and utilize it to our benefit. Focusing on the breath and adopting various sorts of breathing methods – such as Wim Hof breathing or deep, slow belly breaths during meditation – may have good benefits on your mental health.

Your self-care: We can't control the hand we've been dealt in life, and we can't simply "choose" to not have a mental health illness, for example. But the things you can control include how you decide to take care of yourself and your mental wellness – whether that's making a deliberate effort to practice self-care consistently or going to therapy to receive the support you need.

Your diet and fitness: We can't control our genetic predispositions to health disorders or snap out of chronic diseases, but you can concentrate on what you can manage and take command of your physical activity and food. Controlling these parts of your life and having intentional discipline may assist enhance your health.

Use them as ideas for your "Things I Can Control" list and add anything else that relates to you. Keep this list someplace accessible so that you may reference it whenever you feel like your life is out of control, so you can remember that there are always things you can control.

2. Use Mindful Breathing to Focus on What You Can Control

As we discussed, one of the things you can manage is your breath. The breath is a highly powerful tool, and the more you apply conscious discipline to concentrate on your breath, the better you will grow at being able to remain grounded in the present moment and focus on what you can control. Not only will practicing mindful breathing helps you learn to remain focused on things you can control, but it will also offer you additional advantages such as being better able to handle anxiety and stress.

Here is one easy approach to practicing mindful breathing to concentrate on what you can control:

Lay down and lay one hand on your chest and the other hand on your tummy. Take a long, leisurely inhalation through your nose. Remember that breath is one of the things you can manage. Try to inhale for a count of your tummy lift as you breathe in. Hold your breath for a few seconds before exhaling from your mouth via pursed lips, gently and with control. Try to exhale for a count to feel your bell collapse as you breathe out all the air. Continue this method for at least 10 complete breaths. With every inhale and exhale, you might say to yourself, "My breath is one of the many things I can control." Mindful breathing needs conscious discipline, but the more you practice it, the simpler it will grow, and you will undoubtedly experience the advantages.

## 3. CultivatePositivity to Control What You Can Control

When you concentrate on what you can control rather than problems that you can't manage, this helps you build optimism. Think about it: if you concentrate on all the things that are out of your control, you'll undoubtedly feel stressed out and maybe even gloomy. You can feel that things will never change, or you might feel trapped. On the other hand, if you use conscious discipline to change your attention to concentrate on what you can manage, you will have a more positive mentality, and feel like you have the ability and strength to control what you can control. Remember, a little bit of optimism can go a long way!

4. Keep a "Can Do Attitude" to assist Focus on What You Can Control

Along with fostering optimism, adopting a "can do attitude" may allow you to concentrate on things you can control, while also actively working towards managing these things. It's one thing to merely think about the things you can control, but it's another to practice the things you can manage. We propose having a look at your "Things I Can Control" list every day and asking yourself what you can do to perform at least one or two of these action items. Keep your can-do attitude no matter whatever item on the list you're referring - whether it's your breathing or your attitude.

It's going to take time to adjust your mentality to concentrate on what you can manage — but persist with it. It will be well worth it. With intentional discipline and a can-do attitude, you can alter your life. If you need some more support, try to concentrate on what you can control and build new healthy habits using our app. You may also accept our 21-day challenge to truly get your life on track. Life is hard at times. Sometimes we don't get what we want, and we lose our job or marriage, or pregnancy. Or ordinary things occurs-the tedium— like being delayed in traffic or a date cancels at the last minute. So many things are out of our control.

Other individuals are out of your control, the traffic is out of your control, whether your parents have dementia or your buddy gets sick. We can't do anything about such problems but concentrate on what we can control.

Own your power. We can manage our mindset when awful things happen to us.

We can be courageous and attempt to become pregnant again or adopt; we can bring our friend who is unwell food, or take her to the doctor, we can let the person cut in front of us in traffic since they may be late, and not allow it to impact our attitude. These things we can control. We can manage the attitude we bring to any scenario, even the supposedly bad ones.

25 things you can control

1. How you speak to your loved ones

2. Who do you choose to spend your time with, How do you spend your time?

4. Whether you go for a stroll in nature or spend time on Facebook

5. How distracted do you allow yourself to be among friends and family, How much do you read?

7. How much do you watch TV

8. How much you write

9. What you consume

10. How thankful you are

11. How much do you workout

12. How much you lean toward life

13. How much clutter do you live with

14. If you seek aid or not

15. How much shopping you do

16. How much sugar do you consume

17. What entertainment do you allow to take up room in your thoughts

18. How long can you hold your breath

19. What sort of love you will accept

20. Whether you own pets or not

21. Your inner conversation—what you say to yourself

22. Your sleeping habits — whether you get enough or too little

23. Whether you weigh yourself

24. How you determine your morning and evening routine

25. Who do you adore?

You get the idea. There are numerous things under your control —concentrate on them.
Too often, we assume life simply occurs to us, but we have numerous ways to consciously invest our time and construct a life we are proud of, a life we value, and a

life we are thrilled to get up to in the morning.

You start by intending it.
Of doubt, there will be hurdles we can't predict and problems we will have to confront, but we are in charge of how we respond to those issues.
In every challenge that comes up in life, we do have control over how we approach these obstacles; we pick which attitude we bring to situations, and what our perspective is while dealing with circumstances beyond our control.

You are not powerless
You may select how you want to go through anything, moaning non-stop or facing it head-on.
Below are three things you are in control of. When you practice them to the point of mastery, the other stuff — those things which are beyond your control — will be faced with a more strong you equipped with

a mentality to go through them more effortlessly, with more strength and stamina.

Breath/meditation
Breath is life. It focuses on us and roots us; it soothes us and heals us.
I utilize the 4–7–8 breathing pattern to concentrate or when I need to ease anxiety. It's also known as "relaxing breathing." This breathing pattern has been proven to alleviate anxiety as much, if not more, than medicine. It works great.

Here are the steps.

Sit in a comfortable posture.
Place the tip of your tongue on the tissue just below the top of your front teeth. Empty the air in your lungs breathe in through your nose for 4 seconds.
Hold your breath for 7 seconds, Exhale firmly via your mouth for 8 seconds
Repeat at least 4 times

Gratitude

Count your blessings. People who show thanks every day report higher enjoyment in their lives, which may last weeks, and even months. Write a letter to someone you want to express thanks for – you don't even have to mail it. I have written a thankfulness notebook for extended periods of my life, and it has helped me perceive life more favorably. It will raise your attention on what you can manage and is shown to boost happiness.

Every night or every morning, jot down five things you are thankful for.

This activity affects your whole attitude on life; you start to realize, 'Damn, I'm lucky.' Even on days when you cannot think of one thing to be thankful for, you can always recall your breath, and feel appreciation for that. It is not a trivial issue. Breath is life-affirming.

Visualize

Visualize good results in your life. Visualization puts you into an energetic and strong mentality. By concentrating on good ideas, you produce a sense of contentment and thankfulness that remains with you throughout the day. I normally do this at night when I rest my head on the pillow – assuming I can stay up long enough. Visualizing positive occurrences, plans for the future or a nice recollection from the past encourages your mind to concentrate on what is good, which minimizes stress. When you make an effort to imagine the wonderful stuff, you'll have less bandwidth to think about distressing things, primarily beyond your control, things that most likely won't happen anyhow — like the world burning up.

Don't let your illogical thoughts go rampant, it will rob your attention and productivity. It is a discipline, much like entering into a regular meditation practice. It might take some time to get to a position where you can stop your inner chatter and create a regular practice of managing your mental patterns. But like everything in life, practice, and consistency make for success.

Let go of the rest.
There are three things you can manage every day. Your mindset, your work, and your behaviors. The reality is simple. You are NOT in charge. Not of everything, at least. However, you may concentrate on what is under your power and play the odds. If you concentrate on the things you can control, you will position yourself in the most optimal circumstances, most frequently. By doing that, chances are, things will come out the way you want them more frequently than not.

How Do You Do This?
So, how do you do this? By concentrating on what you can control.
How do you know what you can control? You must start by recognizing the

distinction between what you can control and what you can't. This is crucial. I feel there are three things that you can concentrate on every day to guarantee you're concentrating on what you can manage. These three things are your mindset, your effort, and your actions.

- Keep an optimistic attitude

- Work hard every day

- Ensure your activities are making yourself and others better

If you can complete these three easy things each day, you're focused on areas you can control and that are essential.

Attitude:
Choose to be optimistic. Positivity is contagious. Positivity makes you worth connecting with each day. Be someone who other people look forward to seeing each

day. I dare you to try and be the most excited person you know. See how much this affects others around you in a good manner.

Effort:
Your work ethic doesn't develop overnight. It takes years and years of perfecting your talents and working until you attain your objectives. You get to your objectives by putting in the effort. By sitting at the desk and working hard. I connect this to the age-old conundrum, "How do you eat an elephant?" One mouthful at a time. Show up and do the job and work hard each day, one day at a time. Stack these hard-working days on top of each other and ultimately you organically create your work ethic.

Actions:
You know the Golden Rule. Treat people how you would like to be treated. It is a maxim found in various faiths and popular culture. Align your behaviors with your long-term ideals and beliefs. Go out of your

way to be nice to others around you. Open a door. Give a compliment. Ask someone how they're doing—and honestly listen to their response. Take someone out to lunch. You'll be astonished at how these acts of kindness will improve your life. Focus on what you can control to guarantee your life turns out the way you desire. There might be a lot of factors in your life and you can't control many of them. Focus on what you can control and watch your life transform. I guarantee it's not a cliché, it's the reality.

What about you? Will you start concentrating on these three areas to transform your life for the better?

# Chapter 3

## Directing Your Mind to Change

Society doesn't generally accept this viewpoint — but it's OK to alter your opinion. It's frequently a clear indicator that you're developing and working on your objectives.

If you never alter your view about anything, it may suggest that you're not living. Or that you simply aren't willing to learn anymore.

I used to feel that regularly changing my mind about what I wanted to accomplish indicated that there was something wrong with me. Friends and relatives would chastise me: "you can't be continually changing your mind!" Or providing advice: "just choose anything — anything — and stick to it."

There was a time I believed their statements and I felt I needed to mend myself to live my life properly. The good news is that you don't need to believe this. Because what would you rather do: remain with doing something you don't love for the rest of your life – or change your mind?

You Don't Have to Embrace Other People's Beliefs as Your Own.
Chances are you've been informed that changing your opinion often isn't useful. It leads to incomplete initiatives, broken confidence, and squandered money. It's also a symptom that you don't know what you want in life, you're inconsistent and you can't handle the repercussions of your acts. Not exactly the best forecasts for your future. Or so they tell you.

Why Changing Your Mind Is Necessary

In Polish, there is a proverb suggesting that "only cows don't alter their minds." That is to argue that people do and should. Especially individuals who are in love with life and want to make the most of it.

I recognize now that what other people considered altering my mind was only an outward reflection of my interior process. This method was all about finding out the greatest way to live my life by pursuing my interests.

Changing your mind isn't an indication that there's anything wrong with you or that you're setting yourself up for failure. Things only a societal tendency to perceive it this way. In truth, altering your thoughts is only a mirror of all the internal changes going on inside of you. It's more of a consequence than a cause.

"I questioned why altering one's thinking is frequently so difficult. After all, both the world and our vision of it are continually changing; situations never stay static, so why should our answers to them be permanently fixed in their original form?

The fact is that everyone needs to alter their viewpoint once in a while. Otherwise, you'd be now stuck with the choices you made when you were five! A lot has happened in your life since then – therefore your choices and opinions inevitably shift, too.

From this viewpoint, the velocity at which you're changing your mind might be regarded as a consequence of the pace at which you're developing. The more fresh data you accumulate via your experience, the more intricate the picture of your life develops. As this occurs, the vision for your future organically adapts. Some people call it "changing your mind."

But you might term this procedure differently. Now that we looked into what "changing your mind" truly means, we can seek a more acceptable vocabulary to explain it.

"Changing Your Mind" vs "Adjusting Your Vision"

The words we choose to describe our lives matter. Language impacts the way we understand our experiences. Therefore, the word I like to use instead of "changing your mind" is "adjusting your vision." It transforms the way we understand ourselves and our decisions in the context of building the life we desire.

Changing your mind indicates that you feel lost, and undecided and that you rely mainly on external factors to navigate your life.

Adjusting your view shows that there is a constant aim underlying all your activities. It doesn't matter if you don't recognize it consciously yet – the purpose is always there. The act of altering your view is a component of finding this goal. But how does altering your eyesight play out in real life?

Adjusting Vision Is Inevitable in Pursuing Your Dreams

Because you're still reading this essay, I presume that going after your aspirations is essential to you. You may perhaps already have an idea of how to achieve it.

But do I feel that there's still something holding you back?

For most of us, this something is fear. Not only the fear of failing and not being good enough. It's also the worry of having to adjust your plans. The concern is that it may be essential to adapt your vision and let go of control occasionally. This dread is normal, but also feasible to conquer. In essence, all it takes is one choice – to simply do it. Once you've tried the waters long enough, you start trusting in your ability to swim. And if you can swim, you're ready to go offshore and leave the future open, confident that you'll be able to go across the lake. Even if a current knocks you off track – that's alright. You can't plan for it in advance, but you know you're a strong enough swimmer to respond to the circumstances. There's always a way to modify it. In reality, there are infinite methods. Occasionally it will be struggling against the waves and sometimes – letting the ocean take you when the wind blows too fiercely. But you will only be able to see what you need to accomplish once you've left the coast. Once you take the plunge, bear in mind that the alterations to your route are merely that - adjustments. They don't indicate you're abandoning your initial concept. They don't mean you're messing up. All you're doing is refining your vision as you obtain more knowledge, experience, and clarity on your objectives. Adjusting your vision is an indication that you're actively pursuing it. That you're learning from your errors. That you're being open and adaptable.

You may name it as you like. On the surface, it may appear like you're "changing your mind" all the time. But as long as you know what you're dedicated to — or you're actively attempting to uncover it — these shifts are positive.

So don't be frightened to change. Leave the coast, swim as well as you can, and ready yourself to modify the route.

I would argue that changing your opinion is not a sin or a crime or a mistake. It does not make you weak, reckless, and unpredictable.

Your unique life experiences nearly always compel you to modify your perspective, and some of the positives include:

- Avoid rigidity in your thinking.

- Learning new things to make your life more pleasant.

- Keeping your brain healthy by choosing to think differently.

Variety is required to prevent staleness of ideas and mental insufficiency.

Changing your thoughts helps you to have new viewpoints and innovative discoveries. It may lead you to open the door to new possibilities.

Some individuals won't appreciate the thought that you should alter your views; they may even attempt to generate guilt in you about your daring new selections to pursue a different road. But to progress continually, you have to keep altering your thinking.

Doing tough new activities helps increase your confidence to manage any changes that may come your way in the future.

Making substantial changes in life might be intimidating, yet bold and self-aware individuals do it all the time.

It urges you to live on the edge of moral borders and the newest breakthroughs in science and philosophy.

Our capacity to modify our views is principally responsible for steering our whole route of development, from chimps to homo sapiens, from primal cravings to high aspirations, from modest essentials to opulent accessories.

The most essential thing is to embrace the concept that changing your opinion is alright. Tasting new delights of life are not possible if you do not adjust your preconceived views of the world around you.

Key facts about your brain
Shaped by evolution, notably in emotional and relational skills; for example, the greater the primate social group, the bigger the brain. 3 pounds, 1.1 trillion cells, including 100 billion "gray matter" neurons Always "on" – 2 percent of the body's weight utilizes roughly 25 percent of its oxygen. The average neuron contains roughly 5000 connections (synapses), 500 trillion in all Synapses fire 1 to 100 times a second; quadrillions of synapses activate per minute, with brain areas connected by neuronal pulses synchronized within a few milliseconds.

Highly linked network consisting of circular loops: awareness of awareness Number of potential brain states: followed by a million zeros The most complicated item known in the cosmos

Your thinking transforms your brain.

Both momentarily, in electrochemical waves lasting a few milliseconds, and permanently, as existing synapses become reinforced and new ones are formed. As circuits become utilized, they strengthen their connections; "neurons that fire together, wire together."

Your experience counts, leaving an indelible mark behind.
Mindfulness and concentration practices stimulate distinct areas of the brain. Your brain transforms your mind. Brain activity creates mental activity (usually perpetually beyond consciousness) (mostly forever outside awareness). Trauma decreases the hippocampus, which becomes less able to develop new memories. More active left frontal lobes nurture good feelings. You may utilize your thoughts to modify your brain to change your mentality for the better.

- Trigger patterns of neuronal pulses that create calm alertness

- Activate positive emotion pathways, developing resilience and resistance to depression

- Increase serotonin, a chemical that improves mood, sleep, and digestion

- Thicken the anterior cingulate, enhancing attention and self-observation

- Thicken the insula, enhancing internal sense and empathy for others

- Stimulate the parasympathetic nervous system (PNS) for calm well-being

- Strengthen the immune system, promote cardiovascular health, and lessen chronic pain.

# Chapter 4

**Overcoming Destructive Behavior And Habits**

"I am frequently challenged with being aware while purchasing food. What do you do when you are doing things that are self-destructive and are not good and continue to do them? Is there a chance to change this?"

This is such a wonderful question since I believe we can all connect to this, can't we? Who among us doesn't undertake self-destructive habits from time to time, if not daily? I know that I've spent much of my life doing things I wish I didn't do, and only in the past 8-9 years have I (slowly) been able to modify those habits.

So can you modify self-destructive behaviors? Can you stop yourself from doing things you can't seem to stop?

And believe me, I'm no superhuman. I could look disciplined and a model of self-mastery to an outsider, but from inside I have always felt undisciplined, a procrastinator, with a marked lack of self-control. I never imagined I could make changes, but I did.

What worked? Here's the lowdown: a brief guide on modifying these habits when you're having problems.

- Feel the anguish. We don't tend to make adjustments unless we are driven to do so. Sometimes witnessing other individuals make adjustments offers us motivation. But sometimes we simply need to be in an unpleasant spot that we'd prefer to get out of. And so, if you're in that unpleasant position, allow yourself to experience the anguish, and ask yourself if it's time for a change. Eating out of control? Well, what type of pain is this giving you? What do you want to do about it? Get away from that awful area.

- Turn toward the issue. One of the major issues in making life changes is that we prefer to avoid thinking about the problem. It becomes worse and worse, and yet we divert ourselves, since staring at the situation may be terrifying and terrible. But this merely makes the situation worse. If you want to break out of the loop, you have to let yourself think about it. Look at the issue. Acknowledge it. Accept that that's the way it is, with the awareness that it may change, if you recognize it.

- Pick one minor, distinguishing modification. Once you're ready to start making modifications, simply choose one. If you want to modify your eating, you can't do it all at once. It's not practical. So select one change, and be specific: eat one fruit at lunch each day. Drink unsweetened green tea instead of that Big Gulp of soda you had in the afternoon. Drink unsweetened coffee with a dash of creamer instead of a Starbucks large latte with extra whipped cream. Work on resisting going back for seconds until you've taken a 10-minute pause following your first helping. And so forth. One change at a time, slowly.

- Commit big time. While you want your change to be little, you want your commitment to be great. This is what keeps you going when you don't feel like sticking to it. How can you commit to the big time? Announce to a hundred people, or a thousand, that you're going to do something, and ask them to keep you responsible. Join an accountability group. Publicly commit to a major humiliating penalty if you fail. Do it publicly for someone else, or a charitable organization, so you have people you don't want to let down. Make a vow to someone you love. Put a significant quantity of money on it with your pals. Be all in.

- Learn to think that you can. In the beginning, you may undoubtedly have doubts that you can keep to this adjustment. That's OK – start on it anyhow. Stick to it for one modest step (drink a glass of water, eat one fruit), and realize that you can accomplish it. Then stick to it for another modest step. Each time you accomplish it, consider this as proof that you are competent.

- Use failure to learn. While performing the habit is proof that you can do it, failing should not be evidence that you can't. Use it as a chance to learn: learn about how you work best, how habits function, about negative self-talk (see next item), and cravings. Learn about inevitable barriers and how to get through them. Each time you goof up, this is a fantastic chance to grow better, to enhance your approach. Failure isn't a terrible thing – it's fresh knowledge to enhance your habit technique.

- Don't believe the negative self-talk. There will be ideas in your brain about not being able to do it or wanting to stop. Don't listen to them. See them, recognize them, but don't obey their demands or believe what they say. They only come up because your brain is attempting to get out of hard labor. Lazy brain, lying brain. Instead, come up with superior counterarguments: "Brain: You can't do this." "You: Actually, I can and have. Other individuals have done this, and so can I. And I shall only truly know if I try."

- Find support. Ask your spouse or close friend, family, or the Internet, to support you. Ask them to check on you and not let you fail. If you don't have someone supportive near you, locate a group online.

- Create the proper positive & negative feedback. When you consume junk food, it has positive feedback (it's tasty), and there's negative feedback for not eating the junk food (cravings and hunger and wishing you could eat it) (cravings and hunger and wishing could eat it). This is the inappropriate feedback cycle for the change you wish to make. Instead, develop a new feedback loop that supports your modification. More about this is below.

Creating the Right Environment

When you bring all the measures above together, it's about having the ideal atmosphere. Think of it as a greased slope – right now, the slope is greased toward your self-destructive habit, so even if you struggle against it, you're likely to keep performing the activity.

You can intentionally modify the slope. Create your own greased slope, such that it's geared in the direction you want to travel in. For example, if you're attempting to modify the way you eat, get rid of all the junk food in your home, so it's hard to obtain the bad things. Tell folks in your home not to allow you to go to the supermarket or fast food establishments to buy junk. Instead, have healthful food handy for when you're hungry. Have responsibility and repercussions, so that you don't want to humiliate yourself by messing up (negative feedback) and you want to appear good by performing well (positive feedback) (positive feedback). Don't meet folks at locations with bad meals — that's like going to the bar when you're an alcoholic. Give yourself prizes, like a massage, if you stick to it for a week or two. These are simply samples, of course, you'll want to build up your environment for whatever works for you. This is something you can alter over time, which is why failure is such a valuable learning tool: you can identify where your environment needs to be modified. If you linger on your computer instead of exercising, disconnect the computer and give the cable to a buddy to keep until you exercise. And so on, tweaking each time you fail until your environment is set up so you will succeed.

How To Break A Habit

It is tough to shed repetitive types of behavior, particularly when they bring a sort of comfort and relief. But certain behaviors might be unhealthy and even hamper your everyday life. In rare situations, they might also have a detrimental influence on individuals around you. Luckily, it's never too late to conquer them.

Here are a few techniques for leaving bad behaviors behind.

## Get Motivated

The first step in eliminating a harmful habit is having the resolve to do so. If you are set in your ways when it comes to particular habits and hesitant to make adjustments, chances are you won't be successful in defeating them. Discern what the advantages of giving up particular behaviors are. Remember, a habit doesn't just apply to physical traits, like fidgeting, it also extends to acts, like as constantly being late for work or consistently adopting a negative outlook.

## Recognize the Reason

Bad habits are difficult to overcome because they are established actions that we automatically resort to when specific conditions happen. Identifying what fires perpetual kinds of behavior is a crucial step in defeating it. Do you find yourself chewing your nails when you're anxious? Are you more prone to procrastinate when you're stressed? Recognize the conditions and feelings that signal the activities you'd want to put a stop to.

Find a Replacement

If you gain a solid grasp of why you find consolation in certain regular reactions, you may begin to come up with other coping techniques. For instance, take a calming bath after a laborious day instead of eating excessively in front of the TV. Can't quit cracking your knuckles? Try taking a deep breath or short meditating.

Choose a Strategy

It is important to decide how you'd like to go about altering the behaviors. Do you think it would be best to quit cold turkey? Would you rather attempt to slowly limit the amount of time you take comfort in it? For example, if you'd want to quit browsing the internet for extended amounts of time, consider allotting yourself an hour or two each day to browse the web. As time goes by, decrease that period to just one hour.

Define your inclinations. It is crucial to first identify the exact habits you participate in that you believe are damaging to you before trying to modify them. Self-destructive activities might be anything that hurts your physical self or your mind. Compile a list of all of your self-defeating habits that you'd want to modify.

Any of the following qualify as self-destructive behaviors: self-harm (cutting, picking, hitting/punching, scratching, hair-pulling), compulsions (gambling, overeating, substance use, risky sex, excessive shopping), neglect (not paying attention to your needs, health, refusing help), and thoughts/behaviors that cause psychological harm (pessimism, being overly needy, denying responsibility, allowing others to treat you poorly) (pessimism, being overly needy, denying responsibility, allowing others to treat you poorly). There are too many forms of self-destructive habits to mention them all here, so endeavor to study your life and actions for any inclinations that you have that injure you in some manner.

Do you drown your humiliation, sorrow, and guilt by succumbing to substance use and abuse, such as alcohol or drug misuse, or nicotine use?

Write down all of the particular self-destructive patterns that you have. You may maintain a notebook and list each one there.

If you are confused about what some of your habits could be, ask family members or friends if they can point out any behaviors that they believe you perform that are possibly detrimental. Understand why you participate in self-destructive activities. Some research implies that people may engage in self-injurious actions to distract themselves from uncomfortable thoughts or feelings. For each self-destructive behavior, you have put down, explain why you indulge in this activity. For example, there are various reasons you would drink alcohol to excess such as: trying to fit in, feeling insecure, wanting to relax or relieve tension, and wanting to have fun. Think about how the action helps you.

Determine the implications. Identify why each activity is bad. For example, if you discover that your alcohol usage is destructive, highlight the unpleasant things that have occurred in the past when you drank too much. This list may include: blacking out, feeling hungover, making terrible judgments, harming the ones you love, and indulging in unlawful activities. Write down how you feel after dealing with these consequences such as angry, sad, guilty, or shameful.

Track your behaviors. Keep a journal of when you engage in self-destructive actions. Identify the experience, as well as your thoughts, emotions, and acts (whether self-destructive or not) (whether self-destructive or not). Simply maintain a journal of any self-destructive activities you participate in and see what patterns of events, ideas, and emotions arise.

For example, if smoking cigarettes is one of your self-destructive behaviors your list might include positives such as it helps calm you down and is relatively social, and negatives might involve issues such as significant risks to your health, the addictive nature of cigarettes, the high cost of cigarettes, and medical costs.

Identify the benefits of making a change. Based on your evaluation of your self-destructive tendencies, list the advantages and drawbacks of altering each issue habit. This will help you determine which actions are most essential to emphasize.

Accept responsibility. Sometimes we may blame others instead of looking at how we contribute to our self-destructive behavior. It might be challenging to cope with underlying pain due to a bad upbringing or a problematic marriage when abuse patterns are widespread, but we can take charge of our own life by addressing our emotional challenges, healing ourselves, and conquering our addictions.

Identify problematic thought processes. Our ideas seem to be related to our moods and activities. In order words, our views of ourselves and the environment govern how we feel and behave. These ideas are central to Cognitive Behavioral Therapy (CBT), a type of treatment that is commonly used to treat self-destructive behaviors. Write down the ideas that you connect with each of your self-destructive actions. Ask yourself, "What do I think immediately before I do this? What beliefs impact and perpetuate this behavior?" For example, if alcohol usage is the issue, one could believe, "I'll only have one drink. I truly need this drink. I deserve to drink. Nothing horrible will happen." These are the ideas that motivate a person to use alcohol.

Acknowledge your negative thought tendencies. Some of these might include: catastrophizing (thinking the worst will happen), over-generalizing (also known as black and white thinking, where one tends to think something is either all good or all bad), mind-reading (thinking you know what others are thinking), and predicting the future (thinking you know what will happen) (thinking you know what will happen). For instance, if you believe that another person is thinking something awful about you, this might result in you feeling sad or angry, which could spark self-destructive actions. If you adjust this thinking you can avoid the unpleasant feeling and conduct.

Alter your self-destructive ideas. If we modify our thinking, our emotions and actions will follow. Once you have a complete list of the thoughts, you can begin to challenge these thoughts when they come up.

Keep a thinking journal. Identify the scenario, emotion, and thinking. Then identify concepts that support the belief, and ideas that do not support the thought. Finally, utilize this knowledge to develop a more realistic idea. For example, if the event involves your mother shouting at you, you could have felt irritated, and thought, "She's the worst mother." Ideas that support this view may be: she screams, and she doesn't know how to speak gently. Ideas that oppose this notion can be: she tells me she loves me, she gives me food and lodging, she supports me, and so on. A more balanced view overall (to contradict the impression that she is the worst mother) may be, "My mother has her flaws and she does shout occasionally, but I know that she is trying to assist and that she loves me." This thinking may lead to less anger, and hence, better behavior (instead of consuming alcohol or socially isolating) (instead of drinking alcohol or socially isolating).

Practice, practice, practice. Once you understand your problematic thinking and establish alternate beliefs, you need to practice altering these thoughts when they come up. Be conscious of any bad feelings you have (anger, sorrow, tension), and identify the thoughts you are thinking in the present.

You may look back to your thinking journal to aid you. Then, actively change the thought you are having. If you are thinking, "My mother is nasty and doesn't love me," recall the alternative idea you recognized previously and say it to yourself over and over, "My mother loves me although she occasionally loses her anger."

Log your progress and learn from errors. Continue to maintain a record of circumstances that might lead to self-destructive actions. If you detect negative ideas, jot down alternate concepts that could bring a better result. If self-destructive conduct was utilized, identify an alternative. For example, if the circumstance was your mother shouting at you, you may have thought, "I can't tolerate her. She doesn't care about me," followed by sentiments of wrath and resentment, followed by a habit of shutting yourself in your room and withdrawing from social interaction for many days. Identify another method you may have thought of and react to the circumstance. For instance, you may edit the thinking to, "I love her despite her shortcomings, and I know she cares about me even when she behaves this way." Try to ponder such things the next time the event arises (your mother shouts) (your mother yells). Then, you may feel better and strive to reconcile instead of participating in a self-destructive activity. Understand the link between emotions and behaviors. Strong negative emotions such as fear, anxiety, and anger can lead to self-destructive behaviors. Finding new ways of coping with these triggers is crucial to reducing self-destructive behaviors.

Do some deep reflection. More than likely, some triggers precipitate your self-destructive patterns. Use the activities in the previous step to identify thoughts, feelings, and situations that trigger self-destructive tendencies. These will include not just your feelings, but the specific situations which seem to coincide with self-destructive behaviors.

Actively avoid situations that trigger you. For instance, if you want to reduce your drinking, but you know that if you hang out with certain people that will try to pressure you to drink alcohol, avoid this situation altogether. Instead of putting yourself in a potentially risky situation where it may be difficult to say no, give an excuse or explain that you are in recovery.

Make a list of your coping skills. Is important to understand how to cope with these triggers (situations, emotions, and thoughts) to self-destructive behaviors. In addition to modifying your thinking, you may also actively change your self-destructive behavior or replace it with a new activity that is more helpful in helping you cope. Try speaking with your higher power, if you believe in a power greater than yourself. Sometimes, we need to speak about something to let go of it. Try new activities. Find alternatives to your self-destructive behaviors that don't cause more harm than good. For example, you may try: writing, drawing, coloring, sports, camping, hiking, strolling, collecting things, helping people, or gardening.

Tolerate the emotion. Avoid trying to immediately escape an emotion.

 Focus on longer-term healing instead of on instant gratification. Distress tolerance is about learning to cope with emotions instead of merely attempting to avoid experiencing them. Emotions are a fundamental aspect of existence. When you sense a strong negative emotion (anger, despair, stress, frustration), instead of immediately attempting to divert yourself or make yourself feel better in some manner, say to yourself, "I am experiencing _______, and this is a normal sensation to have. Although it is uncomfortable, it won't kill me, and it will pass." Our emotions give us valuable information about how to deal with the current situation. Try thinking about why you are feeling that emotion and what it is telling you. For example, if you are feeling very angry at your mother for yelling at you, identify why you are so mad. Is it because you are hurt by her words, because you think it is inappropriate, or perhaps because you are worried she might do something violent?

Focus on how it feels in your body to feel that emotion. If you feel angry, do you feel tightness in your shoulders, does your body shake, do you clench your fists or teeth? Experience the emotion fully even though it is uncomfortable to do so. Thinking about exactly how it feels in your body can help to take away some of the power of the emotion. After all, feelings are just feelings.

Use writing as therapy. Write down your thoughts and feelings that lead to self-destructive behaviors.

Take care of your health. Sometimes stress can cause us to engage in unhealthy behaviors to cope such as: eating junk food, not exercising, and sleeping less.

Get enough sleep. Most people require at least 8 hours of sleep per night to function optimally.

Eat and drink healthfully. Avoid overindulging in snacks, sweets, or junk food.

Exercise to deal with unpleasant feelings such as stress and sadness.

Engage in healthy relationships. Insecure attachment in relationships is correlated with a higher degree of self-destructive behaviors. Social support is particularly vital to the healing process of self-destructive habits. Identify solid ties you have with family, friends, and other relationships and nurture these connections.

Focus on having great encounters with your loved ones. Spend time with these persons by dining together, exercising, chatting, strolling, playing a game, or attempting a new activity. If you have people in your life who are not supportive or who are abusive toward you, consider detaching or getting space from these individuals. You can start by creating boundaries and explaining to them that you will not tolerate certain behaviors such as yelling at you.

Get help. If you engage in self-harm behaviors this could be associated with depression, anxiety, and aggressiveness. Furthermore, self-destructive behaviors may sometimes be connected to a history of abuse or trauma as well as drug use disorders. Contact a psychologist or therapist. Dialectical behavior therapy (DBT) is a useful treatment for individuals who may have emotional dysregulation or anger, self-harm issues, suicidal thoughts, substance use (alcohol or other drugs), and relationship/interpersonal difficulties. DBT focuses on enhancing your mindfulness, interpersonal effectiveness, emotional control, and distress tolerance. Problem Solving Therapy (PST) helps individuals solve problems better (instead of using self-destructive behaviors) and learn useful coping skills. Cognitive Restructuring (Cognitive Behavioral Therapy-CBT) is about changing your maladaptive beliefs, which helps to reduce negative behaviors.

Explore medication options. Consult a psychiatrist for further information or to explore psychotropic choices.

# Chapter 5

## **Follow Your Intuition**

How To Follow Your Intuition and Why It Matters. keep specialist from The Sleep Centre shows you how to sleep properly and enhance the quality of your life and health.

What is intuition?
As intuition is tough to articulate and delicate in quality, it may easily be ignored completely. However, accessing and obeying the delicate voice of your intuition may be nothing less than life-changing. In this essay, I investigate what the term intuition means and the techniques to connect with it to live more intuitively. Intuition is a word that might make some individuals feel a little uneasy. Sometimes in the discussion, I have found being pushed back with statements like "what does it even mean?" and "Isn't it simply some type of pseudoscience?"

Why is there an increasing interest in intuition?

Despite some opposition, I have lately found that intuition has steadily been more understood by individuals. Often expressed as "I simply get a vibe", "a gut feeling" or "I just knew it from the beginning". Mostly, that's what intuition is - a 'knowing, and insight' or at least faint sensation that anything is incorrect, just right, or possibly requires some more attention.

We might easily overlook the voice of our intuition because of the delicacy of the tone. However, if we can tune in and listen to it, it may impact our lives in ways we never anticipated.

I notice an increase in interest in intuition, a drive among individuals to understand how to feel their instincts and how to trust them. This spike in interest can be partially due to the recent discoveries in science. We now know that intuition is a genuine psychological process in the brain, combining prior experiences and information from the self and the environment to help make up your mind. The choice and feelings frequently happen so rapidly on the subconscious level, that it doesn't register on a conscious level until you have learned to pay attention to them.

Do we all have intuition?
Everyone on the earth possesses intuition, even guys. (Some people ask me whether intuition is exclusive to women!) The main difference among individuals is whether you choose to listen to it or not. You may say that intuition is the way our subconscious mind connects with the conscious mind. In this process, we are getting crucial information that our logical minds cannot access. We now know 'that gut sensation' is true. Having that additional piece of information easily accessible may have a tremendous influence on the decisions we make in our lives.

I have now described what intuition is and why it is so crucial. The following are some of my favorite techniques for you to tune in, and sharpen up that inner knowledge to assist lead you to live an intuitive life.

Three things that might help you listen to your intuition

1. Listen to your inner voice

It may seem so simple, but allowing the mind to slow down to tap into your inner voice is a fantastic method to start hearing your intuition. Ways to achieve this are many: It may be done via meditation, mindfulness, or anything else that allows you to tune in to your inner voice and calm the busy mind. When you hear your intuition make sure you listen to it. Go for it and see what happens.

2. Do not evaluate your emotions or ideas

Turn off the inner critic of your emotions. It is natural to reason away the ideas and feelings within you that don't suit the vision you have of yourself. Instead of turning them off, let your inner conversations flow without criticizing, fearing, or mocking yourself. Just let your emotions be as they are, whatever they are; they are telling you something essential. If you ignore and repress them, it might lead to their rising to the surface later in less beneficial ways. Tuning in to our emotions and bodily response teaches us to understand why we behave and respond in various ways, allowing for more intuitive choices in flow with yourself.

3. Your dreams may hold essential information

Dreams are the brain's method of processing emotional information and interpreting social context. They are filled with vital personal data such as your everyday experiences, your recollections, and things learned during life. Devoting your attention to our dreams may provide you with wonderful knowledge that you may not have access to while awake.

Tip: Before going to sleep, turn your thoughts to any unresolved issues in your life. Go over the possible solutions and options as you're entering the land of dreams. Rest in slumber and let your subconscious do the rest. Make sure to keep a light and cheerful focus on solutions and do not take it too seriously. Keeping things light helps with any worries which may develop.

Have a notepad available beside the bed so that you may jot down your dreams the first thing in the morning.


Living your real potential

To live a life in line with your intuition involves listening to the inner intrinsic knowledge that we all have within us. Once we are completely tuned in, it becomes clearer to see our route in life and sense our purpose. What we can do by living intuitively is beyond our limited conception, yet it is the route by which we may realize our fullest potential.

Intuition: We've all heard of it, but what is it?

Researchers at Leeds University evaluated a large pile of research articles on intuition. They determined that intuition is a very genuine psychological process where the brain utilizes prior experiences and information from the self and the environment to make a choice. The choice occurs so swiftly that it doesn't register on a conscious level. Intuition exists in all of us, whether we recognize it or not. The more we can understand it, the more we can utilize it to alter our lives for the better. The human brain has two 'operating systems. The first is rapid, instinctive, and easy. This is where our intuition resides. Intuition works by drawing on patterns acquired by our experience and when we have to make a rapid judgment about whether something is genuine, false, feels good, feels awful, correct, or wrong, we rely on these patterns. If everything occurs 'offline', beyond our conscious consciousness. The second operating system is slower to react. It's more analytical and purposeful and it's mindful.

The Evidence

Science has uncovered solid evidence to support the existence of intuition. There are many other studies, but let's speak about one in particular - because it's an excellent one. This specific research revealed how the intuitive half of our brain knows the proper answer much before the more analytical section.

In this research, participants played a card game that, unbeknownst to the participants, was rigged from the outset. Participants had to pick from one of two decks of cards. One was rigged to generate enormous winnings, then big losses. The other – tiny profits but seldom any losses.

The participants claimed that after 50 cards, they had an intuition regarding which deck was safer. After 80 they were able to describe the difference between the two decks. But here's where it gets fascinating - after just 10 cards, the sweat glands on the palms of their hands opened whenever they took from the risky deck. It was about then that participants began to favor the safer deck but there was no cognitive knowledge that this was occurring. So, before the analytical half of their brain recognized what was going on, the subjects' intuition directed them towards a better conclusion.

Sharpening Your Intuition
Every individual on the earth possesses intuition but not every person who listens chooses to listen to it. Intuition is the way the subconscious mind connects with the conscious consciousness. The knowledge that informs 'that feeling' is genuine. It's like

any other choice but the workings of it. The gathering, the storage, and the putting together occur outside of our conscious awareness. So intuition is a fantastic thing. The sharper it is, the better off you'll be. Here's how to feed yours so it's blooming and ready to advise.

Shhh. Listen.
It sounds easy enough — and it is. No trickery here. Your intuition can't communicate to you if you're not listening. When you start to take attention, wonderful things will happen. Just try it and see.

Trust your gut intuition.
When a term like 'gut' joins up with a word like 'feeling', you know there has to be a good reason. And there is. Research reveals that emotion and intuition have a physical existence in our stomach. The stomach is lined with a network of neurons and is frequently referred to as the 'second brain.' It's known as the enteric nervous system

(ENS) and it has roughly 100 million neurons, which is more than the spinal cord and peripheral nervous system but fewer than the brain. This is why we become 'sick' about having to make a challenging choice or knowing we've made a terrible one.

Feel.
You'll know your intuition is there because you'll be able to feel it — if you allow yourself. You'll feel it in your gut and it will goosebump your skin, send a chill down your spine, accelerate your pulse and hasten your breath. Sometimes it's even more subtle and the only way to describe it is a 'knowing'. You'll sense when something is correct — it will seem clear, nutritious, and satisfying. And you'll sense when anything is awry — for me, it's an aching or a flatness. Trusting your intuition could be challenging at first if you're not accustomed to it, but give it time and believe it little by bit, if that feels better. It will be worth it.

Be ready to let bad feelings go.
Negative emotions will cloud intuition, which is why when you're angry or depressed bad decisions can happen so easily. Research has backed this, finding that people made better intuitive choices in a word task when they were in a positive mood as compared to when they were in a negative mood.



Be deliberate about the people you hang on to.
People who drain you will add to the noise and make it more difficult to hear what your intuition wants you to hear. Chances are that you already know how they are. If not, be still for a moment – your intuition will be trying to tell you. Keep individuals who nourish and strengthen you and move away from those that deplete you. Understandably, you can't always walk away from the bothersome ones and if that's the

case, empower yourself by making it your decision to remain, rather than not theirs since they've stolen your option. The distinction is slight in phrase but significant in effect. One allows the power remains with you, one passes it over to them.

Pay attention to what's going on around you. The more information you can acquire from the environment, the more the intuitive, subconscious portion of your brain has to deal with – and the more correctly it will guide your judgments.

Connect with others.
There are so many elements that influence our ideas and judgments other than words. Tone, the volume of voice, body language, and gestures - all contribute to the meaning we assign to our encounters with others. Sometimes, we get a sense of individuals but can't exactly put a finger on what it is. People could look distant, preoccupied, or indifferent, and frequently these aren't

voiced but are 'picked up in other ways. The capacity to pick up on the thoughts, emotions, and intentions of another is referred to as 'empathic accuracy. The more time we spend with others, the more we can precisely hone our empathetic accuracy. Being able to pick up the signals of others will all contribute to intuition.

Find time to be quiet and still.
Having isolation lowers the cacophony of the world and helps you to tune in to your intuition. Our intuition is continually providing warnings and encouragement but frequently we are too busy to notice. Let your mind roam and be receptive to anything that comes to you - sensations, ideas, or words. One of the ways to achieve this is via mindfulness. By concentrating your thoughts on your own experience in the present now, mindfulness gets rid of mental clutter and creates a place for you to connect with your intuition.

Ways To Develop & Strengthen Your Intuition

We live in a fear-based society that obsesses on attempting to control life. We're terrified of uncertainty, so we're constantly anticipating everything that might go wrong and doing everything within our power to guard against inevitable disaster. It's an exhausting way to live and can lead to a chronic state of stress, anxiety, and exhaustion. Luckily, you don't need fear to defend you because you have intuition—a strong inner knowledge.

We are all gifted with an intuition that is powerful, trustworthy, and flawlessly attuned to our real path. Whether you utilize it or not is up to you. Here are a few methods to dial up the volume on that trustworthy inner voice:

1. Meditate.

Messages from your intuition tend to be quiet, so spending time in solitude will help you hear and analyze these messages.

2. Get inventive.

Engaging in creative pursuits, such as sketching, scrapbooking, or free-flow writing quiets the cognitive mind and enables your intuition to speak out.

3. Test your hunches.

Got a sense of which horse will win at the track? Getting a sense that it will rain tomorrow even though the weather forecast says it won't? Do you simply know your best friend's new man is terrible news? If you have feelings about what might happen in the future, write down your hunches, then check them later. See how often you were right.

4. Consult your body compass.

Your intuition talks to you via your body, and the more you develop somatic awareness, the more receptive you become. If you experience an unpleasant bodily sensation while you're attempting to make a choice, pay attention. Do you feel light or heavy? Got a terrible sensation in your gut? Saddled with a headache or diarrhea? It might simply be the product of stress reactions caused by mistaken anxiety, but it could also be your intuition ringing loud and clear.

5. Escape from your everyday routine.

Get away. Slow down. Go on a retreat, take a sabbatical, or spend a day in unfamiliar surroundings with nothing scheduled. When you're extremely busy, it's hard to be alert to the gentle words of intuition. Try emptying your schedule and see if your intuition pipes up.

6. Spend time in nature.

Being in the natural environment, away from technology and the cognitive mind's other temptations, may open up the type of intuition we required when we as a species lived outdoors and depended upon it to keep us safe from the weather, predators, and other actual frightening risks.

7. Learn from the past.

Recall a terrible encounter from your history, especially something pretty recent. Before this thing happened, think back to whether you got any feelings that urged you to steer clear. Maybe you received a gut sensation something wasn't right. Maybe you experienced a foreshadowing dream or a vision. If so, did you pay heed to that sensation, dream, or vision, or did you argue yourself out of it? Try to recall precisely how you felt. Recall as many details as possible. The more you can come in touch with the part of you that attempted to warn you, the more you'll trust it next time.

8. Feel more, think less.

The mind thinks, always chattering away, arguing with itself like a crazy person. Intuition, on the other hand, feels. If you're not sure whether you're listening to your fearful mind or your trustworthy intuition, see if you can differentiate whether you're thinking or feeling.

9. Engage in repetitive movement.

Run. Dance. Chop carrots. Play the piano. Paint. These physical actions can calm the cognitive mind and open up your intuition.

10. Align with your values.

Your mind may steer you away from your integrity, but your intuition never will. Become comfortable with how you feel when you're betraying your values, and you'll learn what intuition doesn't feel like. Learn what it feels like to behave in alignment with your values, and you'll start to sense your intuition more clearly.

11. Practice sensing into people before you know them.

See what kind of information you can glean from observing people and feeling their energetic signature before you talk to them or learn anything about them from other people. The more you pay attention, the more you'll realize you already know things you couldn't possibly know with the cognitive mind.

12. Read books about how to develop your intuition.

Try Sonia Choquette's Trust Your Vibes, Shakti Gawain's Developing Intuition.

13. Train your intuition.

You can study intuition in formal classroom settings, as well as in online programs. Try the Academy of Intuition Medicine, the Foundation for Spiritual Development, or Jenai Lane's Spirit Coach training program.

14. Release your resistance.

Don't call yourself crazy when you get an intuitive hunch. Often, the conscious mind disputes with intuition rather than accepting it. By doing this, you may rationalize yourself out of intuitive knowing that could change your life for the better.

15. Start a new breathwork practice.

Breathwork, the purposeful manipulation of the breath, may provide important insights very fast. Try one of these three breathwork techniques for turning inward by way of the breath.

# Chapter 6

## Cognitive Reframing And The Impact Of Happiness

Individuals seek to obtain happiness, although various individuals have varied conceptions of what it is. The majority of persons frequently refer to their present mood or a larger sense of how they feel about life in general when they debate what happiness is.

Definition of happiness: Joy, pleasure, satisfaction, and a feeling of completion characterize the emotional state of happiness. Although there are many various definitions of happiness, it is commonly considered to encompass pleasurable sensations and a sense of satisfaction in one's life.

Since the term "happiness" has such a broad connotation, psychologists and other social scientists prefer to refer to this emotional state as "subjective well-being." Subjective well-being, as the name indicates, largely focuses on how a person feels about their present condition in life.

There are two key factors of happiness (or subjective well-being):

Everyone has a healthy mix of both positive and bad sensations, emotions, and moods. Generally speaking, being happy is related to experiencing more positive experiences than bad ones.

Life satisfaction relates to how pleased you are with various parts of your life, such as your relationships, job, achievements, and other things you value greatly.

The Greek philosopher Aristotle proposed another definition of pleasure, stating that it is the sole human wish and that all other human wants are methods to achieve it. He felt that there were four forms of pleasure:

happiness that came from immediate fulfillment, happiness that came from comparison and success, happiness that came from performing good things, and happiness that came from discovering fullness.

Aristotle believed that the golden mean, which requires maintaining a balance between lack and excess, may lead to happiness.

Happiness Indicators

Even though everyone's ideas of happiness may differ, there are a few essential markers that psychologists look for when assessing and evaluating happiness.

Key markers of happiness include:

having the sense that your life is what you wanted

allowing things to happen as they occur and being receptive to life as it is feeling as though your life is going nicely

enjoying positive, healthful encounters with others

having the belief that your life objectives have been or will be realized

being satisfied with your life

having more joyful than negative sentiments

being sensitive to novel ideas and interactions

Taking care of oneself and being polite and sensitive to oneself

A sense of gratitude

feeling as though your life has significance and is being lived with purpose wish to convey your joy and happiness to others

It's vital to bear in mind that happiness isn't a situation of everlasting joy. Happiness, on the other hand, is the overall experience of having more pleasant than bad sensations.

The complete gamut of human sensations, including irritation, loneliness, boredom, and sadness, may nevertheless impact cheerful folks. But despite their pain, they keep a sense of optimism that things will better, that they can handle the situation, and that they will soon be able to smile once more.

The Advantages of Positivity

Different Kinds of Joy
There are many various viewpoints on what happiness is. For instance, Aristotle, a Greek philosopher, differentiated between two

sorts of happiness: hedonia and eudaimonia.

Hedonia: Pleasure is the source of hedonic joy. It is generally associated with following one's instincts, taking care of oneself, completing objectives, having fun, and feeling satisfied.

Eudaimonia: This form of joy derives from pursuing virtue and importance. Having a feeling of purpose and meaning in life is a fundamental part of eudaimonic well-being. It is more typically associated with carrying out duties, making long-term investments, caring for the welfare of others, and defending personal ideals.

In psychology nowadays, hedonia and eudemonia are more generally referred to as pleasure and meaning, respectively. Psychologists have more recently recommended the introduction of a third element, which is connected to engagement.

These are emotions of passion and participation in numerous parts of life.

According to studies, those who are pleased with their lives tend to score higher than average on both eudaimonic and hedonic life satisfaction scores. Even if the relative relevance of each could vary substantially depending on the person, all of them can contribute significantly to the overall experience of pleasure. While some activities may lean more toward one or the other, others might be equally pleasurable and significant.

For instance, volunteering for a cause you support may be more rewarding than fun. On the other hand, viewing your favorite TV show might score higher on pleasure and lower on significance.

These three basic categories may comprise various forms of happiness, such as:

Joy: A present-moment sensation that is typically simply transient. A cheerful mood that involves awaiting something with favorable anticipation is excitement.

Thankfulness: An uplifting mood marked by gratitude and appreciation. It is a feeling of satisfaction in work or accomplishment. Having an enthusiastic, optimistic view of life is known as optimism.

Contentment is a condition of satisfaction defined by a sense of contentment.

What Kinds of Happiness Are There?

Ways to Foster Happiness
There are things you can do to boost your experience of happiness, even though some people simply have a propensity to be cheerful.

Follow your intrinsic objectives
Achieving goals that you are naturally inspired to strive for, particularly ones that are based on community and personal progress, could aid raise happiness. According to studies, accomplishing these

sorts of internally motivated aims could improve happiness more than reaching extrinsic goals, such as earning riches or reputation.

Take in the Moment
According to research, people typically overearn because they are too consumed with accumulating items to remember to enjoy what they are doing. Therefore, put more effort into fostering an appreciation for the goods you currently have and take joy in the process as you go as opposed to falling into the trap of mindlessly acquiring for the price of your happiness.


Reframe unfavorable ideas
Look for techniques to restate your thoughts more positively when you find yourself in a gloomy mood or feeling pessimistic.
People naturally tend to concentrate more on bad than good things, which is known as

a negativity bias. This may affect everything, including your decision-making process and the way you view other people. Bad thoughts may also be compounded by discounting the good, a cognitive bias in which people accentuate the bad and reject the positive.

It's not about rejecting the bad to reinterpret these thoughts. Instead, it includes seeking to observe events objectively and realistically. It helps you to detect patterns in your thinking and then challenge unpleasant notions.

The impact of happiness
Why does happiness matter so much? It has been demonstrated that happiness may predict beneficial outcomes in a range of life domains, including mental health, physical health, and overall longevity.

Positive sentiments improve life enjoyment.

Happy people have more robust coping methods and emotional reserves.

Positive moods are related to increased health and longer lifespans.

Resilience is increased by good emotions. People with higher resilience are better equipped to deal with stress and recover from setbacks. For instance, one study revealed that those who are joyful commonly have lower cortisol levels and that these benefits often remain over time. People who identify themselves as being in a good mood are more likely to pursue healthy behaviors like eating a balanced diet and exercising regularly.

Being satisfied may help you remain healthy more frequently. Immunity is connected to positive emotional states.

How to Become Happier

According to a large-scale investigation comprising over 2,000 twins, roughly 50 percent of overall life happiness was related to genetics, 10 percent to outside influences, and 40 percent to individual behaviors. Some people appear to have a stronger baseline amount of enjoyment.

There are therefore things you can do to make your life better and more meaningful even though you may not be able to affect what your "base level" of happiness is. Even the happiest individuals occasionally suffer melancholy, hence everyone should actively endeavor to attain happiness.

Develop Powerful Relationships

Being well-adjusted involves social support, which is vital. Good social ties are the greatest indication of happiness, according to a study. Positive and supportive interactions with individuals you care about may work as a stress reduction, boost your health, and make you happy.

Researchers observed that relationships and how satisfied people are in those interactions had a substantial impact on overall health in the Harvard Research of Adult Development, a longitudinal study that tracked participants for almost 80 years.

Building strong social bonds is a good place to start if you want to boost your happiness. Think about enhancing your present friendships and look at techniques to build new ones.

Exercise Frequently

Exercise improves both the body and the mind. A multitude of medicinal and psychological benefits, including greater mood, are related to physical exercise. Regular exercise may help avoid the symptoms of depression, according to multiple studies, but there is also evidence that it may make people feel joyful. Researchers observed a continuously beneficial association between physical activity and happiness in one examination of older data.

Exercise promotes happiness even in modest doses; individuals who exercised even once a week or for only 10 minutes each day reported higher levels of satisfaction than those who never worked out.

Express appreciation
In one study, participants were encouraged to spend 10 to 20 minutes each night before sleep writing. Others were advised to write about tiny irritations, some about insignificant incidents, while still others were told to express their appreciation. According to the results, individuals who wrote about their gratitude experienced an increase in cheerful sensations, increased subjective pleasure, and greater levels of life satisfaction. keeping a thanksgiving notebook is a relatively fast, affordable, simple, and pleasurable way to enhance your mood. Consider setting out a short period each night to reflect on or write down

the things in your life for which you are thankful.

## Why It's Important to Record Your Gratefulness Each Day

### Discover Your Purpose

According to research, those who feel as if their lives have meaning are happier and more contented. Having a sense of purpose is believing that your life has objectives, a direction, and a purpose. Promoting better practices might aid to boost happiness.

You may do the following things to help you discover a sense of purpose:

Investigate your hobbies and interests

Take part in charitable and philanthropic endeavors.

Attempt to correct injustices

Look for novel topics that you may wish to research further.

Many things affect this feeling of purpose, but you can also work to develop it. It entails identifying a goal that is very important to you and will motivate you to take effective, constructive action to go toward that goal.

The Difficulties of Finding Happiness

Even if achieving happiness is vital, there are situations when this aim is not reached. To watch out for are some difficulties:

Putting the Wrong Value on

Although research shows that spending money on experiences rather than material objects would make you happy, money may not be able to buy happiness. According to one study, for instance, spending money on products that save time, like paying for time-saving services, could enhance pleasure and life satisfaction. In contrast to placing an excessive value on things like money, prestige, or material belongings, pursuing objectives that increase the free time or expose one to pleasurable experiences may lead to greater pleasure.

Refusing to Seek Social Support.

Having friends and relatives you can depend on for aid suggests you have social support. According to a study, perceived social support is vital for one's subjective well-being. For instance, one study revealed that 43 percent of a person's happiness was affected by their estimations of social support. It's vital to bear in mind that quality surpasses quantity in terms of social support. Your entire enjoyment will be impacted more by a small group of close friends than by a huge number of casual acquaintances.

Consideration of Happiness as a Goal

Happiness is not a location you can simply travel to and call it a day. It is a continuing activity that requires continual attention and assistance.

According to one study, persons who lay the greatest focus on happiness are also likely to be the least content with their lives. Happiness essentially becomes such a lofty ideal that it nearly becomes unachievable.
"valuing happiness can be self-defeating as the more people value happiness, the more possible it is that they would feel unhappy."
Perhaps the lesson is to avoid placing your eyes on something with such a broad connotation as "happy." Instead, focus on building and cultivating the types of relationships and a life that will make you happy and content.
It's also vital to think about your concept of happiness. A vast notion, happiness may mean diverse things to different persons. Instead of perceiving happiness as a goal, it

may be more advantageous to explore what it means to you before making modest adjustments that might make you happy. As a consequence, attaining these goals may be easy to manage.

Setting Health Goals: How to Do It S.M.A.R.T.

An Overview of Happiness
It has long been understood that happiness is essential to one's health and well-being. The American Declaration of Independence defines the "pursuit of happiness" as an unalienable right. But over time, our idea of what makes us happy has evolved.
A multitude of ideas has been put forth by psychologists to explain how people want and experience happiness. These theories comprise:

Maslow's Theory of Motivation
According to the hierarchy of needs, people are pushed to strive for ever-more

sophisticated demands. People are then motivated by increased psychological and emotional demands once their essential wants have been addressed. The desire for self-actualization, or the impulse to reach one's greatest potential, is at the summit of the hierarchy. The theory also highlights the relevance of transcendent moments or peak experiences when a person feels tremendous understanding, joy, and satisfaction.


Intentional Psychology
Positive psychology is oriented toward the pursuit of happiness. Positive psychologists are interested in identifying techniques that increase optimism and aid people in having better, more satisfying lives. The field tries to develop techniques to aid people, communities, and society in increasing positive emotions and obtaining greater enjoyment rather than focusing on mental diseases.